100 Bible Stories
100 Bible Songs

Created by Stephen Elkins

Illustrated by Tim O'Connor

INTEGRITY®
PUBLISHERS
family

About the Author: S T E P H E N   E L K I N S is president and owner of Wonder Workshop, the third largest independent children's music company in the world (*Billboard Magazine*). A passionate belief in the relevancy of God's Word in everyday life has been the focus and goal of Stephen Elkins's ministry for over 15 years. The fruit of this work has resulted in over 200 Christian books, musicals, audio programs, and videos which, together, have sold over 10 million copies and earned a Grammy nomination.

100 BIBLE STORIES, 100 BIBLE SONGS

Stories and songs written by Stephen Elkins.

Arr ©℗2004 Wonder Workshop, a division of Stephen's Group, Inc., Mt Juliet, TN. All rights reserved. Unauthorized duplication is prohibited by law and the eighth commandment.

All lyrics on website at www.wonderworkshop.com

Published by Integrity Publishers, a division of Integrity Media, Inc. 5250 Virginia Way, Suite 100, Brentwood, TN 37027.

I N T E G R I T Y   P U B L I S H E R S ,   I N C .

HELPING PEOPLE WORLDWIDE EXPERIENCE *the* MANIFEST PRESENCE *of* GOD

Illustrated by Tim O'Connor

Cover and interior design: Russ McIntosh, Brand Navigation, LLC — www.brandnavigation.com

Special thanks to The Wonder Kids Choir: Jonathan Durham, Emily Elkins, Amy Lawrence, Lindsey McAdams, Amy McPeak, Matthew Oxley, and Allie Smith.

Engineer: Randy Moore

Arrangements: John DeVries

ISBN 1591452392

Library of Congress Cataloging-in-Publication Data

Elkins, Stephen.
  100 favorite Bible stories / Stephen Elkins.
    p. cm.
  Summary: "100 Biblical stories for children includes sing a long songs"--Provided by publisher.
  ISBN 1-59145-239-2 (hardcover)
  1. Bible stories, English. I. Title: One hundred favorite Bible stories. II. Title.
  BS551.3.E35 2005
  220.9'505--dc22
  2004026729

Printed in China
05 06 07 08 RRD 9 8 7 6 5 4 3 2

All lyrics to the 100 Bible Songs can be found at *www.wonderworkshop.com*

Presented To

From

Date

Be an example to show the
believers how they should live.

1 TIMOTHY 4:12 ICB

— Table of Contents —

— Table of Contents —

— Table of Contents —

*written by Stephen Elkins   **written by Stephen Elkins & Ron Kingery

Old Testament

Creation

"In the beginning God created the heavens and the earth."

from
GENESIS 1:1-25

God made everything. When God said, "Let there be light," there was light! He called the light day and the dark night. That is what God did on the first day. On the second day, God made the sky. On day three, He made the mountains and oceans. Then He made the trees and flowers. On the fourth day, God made the sun, moon, and stars. On day five, God filled the oceans and lakes with fish. He made the birds and butterflies too. On the sixth day, God made all the animals. God made everything good. But He wasn't finished yet!

God is good.
God made everything good.

I know God is good because of what He made.

Adam and Eve

— GOD MADE ME —

"God made me. In my Bible it says that God made me."

from
GENESIS 1:26-2:25

On the sixth day of Creation, God made the first man. His name was Adam. God also created a beautiful garden called Eden. It was a perfect home with everything he needed. God gave Adam work to do. He was to take care of all that God had made. But Adam was lonely. God said, "It is not good for Adam to be alone. I will make him a helper." So God made a woman. Her name was Eve. Together, Adam and Eve took care of the garden and worshiped God.

God created everything.
God made Adam and Eve.

God made me too!

Temptation for Adam and Eve

—BE CAREFUL LITTLE EYES—

"Oh be careful little ears what you hear, for the Father up above is looking down with love."

from
GENESIS 3:1-6

God said to Adam, "You may eat from every tree in the garden except one." God warned Adam that if he disobeyed, he would die. One day, the evil one appeared in the garden in the form of a snake. He was very clever. He found Eve alone and asked, "Did God really tell you not to eat from this one tree in the garden?" Eve answered, "Yes, He did."

"You will not die!" he said. "Try it!" So Eve looked at the fruit. It looked good to eat. She remembered God's warning. But believing the lie, she took the fruit and ate it. She gave some to Adam too. Adam and Eve disobeyed God.

God always tells the truth,
but Adam and Eve did not listen to God.

I will listen to God.

Leaving Eden

"It's me, it's me O Lord, standing in the need of prayer."

from
GENESIS 3:8-23

Adam and Eve heard the voice of God calling, "Adam, where are you?" Adam answered, "We're hiding because we're afraid." Then God asked, "Adam, did you eat the fruit I told you not to eat?" Adam answered, "Eve gave me the fruit. She ate it first." Then God said, "Eve, what have you done?" She said, "The evil one tricked me. He told me I would not die! He told me I would be as wise as You are!" Adam and Eve were ashamed of what they had done. They had disobeyed God. Then God said to the evil one, "You have done a bad thing." God told Adam and Eve, "Now, you will have to leave Eden and work very hard." It was a very sad day.

16

Disobeying God causes trouble.
Adam and Eve disobeyed God
and had to leave the garden.

I will obey God and receive His blessings!

Noah Builds the Ark

—WHO BUILT THE ARK?—

"Who built the ark? Noah! Noah!"

from
GENESIS 6

Noah was a good man living in a bad time. All the other people had become mean and unkind. They didn't love God at all. All they thought about was doing mean things.

That made God very sad. But Noah and his family loved God. This made God happy. God told Noah to build a big boat called an ark. He said there would be a flood and all the earth would be covered with water. Noah and his family would be safe on the ark. God would send animals to Noah so they could be safe too.

Loving God makes Him happy.
Noah loved God.

I will love God.

Noah's Big Boat

—NOAH'S ARKY ARKY—

"The Lord said to Noah, 'There's going to be a floody, floody.'"

from
GENESIS 6-7

God brought two of every kind of animal to the ark. In came two tigers. Can you find a cat? In came two giraffes. Can you find a giraffe? Then God closed the door. The thunder crashed! BOOM! The lightning flashed! ZOOM! The animals were so afraid! It rained for forty days and forty nights. Floodwaters covered the whole earth. But Noah's ark floated upon the waves. Up and down went the great big boat. At night Noah could hear the sounds of all the animals. But Noah's family and the animals didn't mind. They were safe in the ark! There were antelope, buffalos, cats, dogs, elephants, and foxes. Can you name some other animals aboard Noah's ark?

God keeps us safe.
Noah obeyed God and was saved from the flood!

I will trust God to keep me safe.

Noah's Rainbow

—A TO Z WITH NOAH—

"We're going A to Z with Noah and the animals in the ark."

from
GENESIS 8—9:17

The rain stopped. When the land dried up, Noah, his family, and all the animals came out of the ark. Noah thanked God for keeping them safe. God put a beautiful rainbow in the sky to show He would never again flood the whole earth. It was a beautiful day!

A rainbow is a sign of God's promise.
Noah thanked God for sending the rainbow.

When I see a rainbow,
I will remember God's promises to me.

Father Abraham

—FATHER ABRAHAM—

"Many sons had Father Abraham. I am one of them and so are you."

from GENESIS
12:1-4; 15:5-6; 21:1-5

One day, God spoke to Abraham, "Leave your country and go to a land I will show you. I will bless you and make your family into a great nation." Abraham obeyed God. One night, God told Abraham, "Look at the sky. There are so many stars you cannot count them. You will have so many children that you won't be able to count them all." Abraham was puzzled. He and his wife Sarah were very old and had no children. But Abraham believed God. Later, when Abraham was 100 years old, Sarah had a baby boy, just as God had promised. They named him Isaac.

Nothing is too hard for God.
Abraham believed God.

I will believe what God says.

Abraham and Isaac

—ROCK MY SOUL—

"Rock my soul in the bosom of Abraham."

from GENESIS 22:1-13

Abraham and Sarah loved their son, Isaac. One day, God decided to test Abraham to see how much Abraham loved God. God said, "Abraham, take Isaac and give him back to Me." That made Abraham very sad. But he trusted God to do the right thing. Together, Abraham and Isaac climbed a steep mountain. Isaac said, "Father, I don't understand." Abraham answered, "God will provide." Suddenly an angel called out, "Abraham! You do not have to give your son back to God. Now God knows you love Him more than anything. You love God even more than you love your son, Isaac. Because you trusted God, you and your family will be blessed more than all people."

God wants us to love Him more than anything.

Abraham loved God and offered
to give Isaac to Him.

I will love God more than anything.

A Wife for Isaac

—THE PLANS I HAVE FOR YOU—

"For I know the plans I have for you my little children."

from
GENESIS 24:1-22

Isaac grew up. His father, Abraham, sent his servant to find Isaac a wife. As he came to the town, he stopped at a well. He asked God to help him find Isaac a wife: "When the girls come to get water from the well, guide me to Isaac's wife. Let her give me a drink, and then let her offer water for my camels too." Just then, Rebekah came carrying a water pot. She gave him a drink from her water pot. She said, "Here is water for your camels too." He knew Rebekah was God's choice for Isaac.

God guides those who pray.

Abraham's servant prayed and God guided him.

I will pray for God to guide me.

Twins for Rebekah

—COUNT YOUR BLESSINGS—

"Count your blessings, name them one by one.
And it will surprise you what the Lord has done."

from GENESIS
25:21-34

Isaac and Rebekah were about to become parents. But even before her babies were born, God told Rebekah her twins would be very different. "One will be stronger than the other. The older brother will serve the younger." When the babies were born, they were such a blessing. She was thankful God answered her prayers! The oldest twin, Esau, was red and hairy. The younger twin, Jacob, had fair hair and smooth skin. Esau grew up to be a skillful hunter. Jacob stayed close to home. When they grew up, Jacob, the younger brother, received the blessing of his father, Isaac. Esau served him, just as God had said.

Be thankful for God's many blessings.

Rebekah was thankful for Jacob and Esau.

I will have a thankful heart.

Jacob's Ladder

—WE ARE CLIMBING JACOB'S LADDER—

"We are climbing Jacob's ladder, soldiers of the cross."

from
GENESIS 28:10-22

Jacob was on a long journey. As night came, he stopped to rest. He spread his blanket across the ground and used a large stone for a pillow. While he was sleeping, he had a dream. He saw a stairway leading up to heaven. The bottom of the stairway rested on the ground. The angels of God were climbing up and down the stairway. At the top of the stairway was God. He said to Jacob, "I will watch over you. I will be with you wherever you go." And Jacob promised he would trust God.

God watches over us.
Jacob trusted God.

I will trust God to watch over me.

Joseph's Coat

—JOSEPH'S COAT OF MANY COLORS—

"Many colors, Joseph had a coat of many colors."

from
GENESIS 37:1-11

Years passed and Jacob had twelve sons.
Joseph was the youngest. One day, Jacob gave
Joseph a special coat of many beautiful colors.
Jacob did not give his other sons a special coat.
His brothers were very jealous of Joseph. Then
God sent Joseph important dreams. Joseph told
his brothers about them. Joseph's brothers did
not like his dreams and were angry. One day
one brother said, "When Joseph brings our food,
let's get rid of him." "Let's throw him into a pit,"
another said. Then they had another idea. They
sold Joseph as a slave to some traders. But God
took care of Joseph.

God is with us, even in the bad times.
He was with Joseph when his
brothers sold him as a slave.

In hard times I know God is with me.

Joseph Forgives

from
GENESIS 37, 44, 45

The traders took Joseph far away to Egypt. But God took care of Joseph. The king of Egypt saw how wise Joseph was and how hard he worked. He made Joseph an important leader. He put Joseph in charge of all the grain in the land. One day, all of Joseph's brothers came to Egypt to ask for food. They were afraid when they saw Joseph because they didn't know what he would do to them for selling him.

But Joseph forgave his brothers and gave them the food they needed. Then his whole family moved to Egypt. His father, Jacob, was happy to see his son again.

God tells us to forgive others.

Joseph forgave his brothers.

I will forgive others.

Baby Moses

—HE'S GOT THE WHOLE WORLD IN HIS HANDS—

"He's got the whole world in His hands."

from
EXODUS 2:1-10

Jacob's family grew in number. The new king in Egypt did not like them. One day, an Israelite woman had a baby boy. Since the king was so mean, she wanted to hide her baby from him. She made a special basket that would float in water. Carefully, the mother put her baby in the basket. She set it in the river among the tall grass. An Egyptian princess saw the basket floating in the water. When she found the baby boy, she loved him. The princess decided to keep the baby. She named him Moses. Moses's sister was watching nearby and said, "I can find a nurse to take care of the baby." And she brought Moses's own mother to care for him. God took care of baby Moses.

God watches over us all.
He kept baby Moses safe.

God watches over me and will keep me safe.

The Bush that Wouldn't Burn

—MY GOD IS SO BIG—

"My God is so big, so strong and so mighty, there's nothing my God cannot do!"

from
EXODUS 3:1-10

Moses was once a prince in Egypt. But he broke the law defending an Israelite slave. So Moses ran far away and became a shepherd. One day God spoke to him in a very odd way. Before Moses was a bush that burned with a brilliant flame. But the bush did not burn up! God spoke from the bush saying, "Moses, take off your sandals. This is holy ground!" Then He told Moses, "Go back to Egypt and tell the Pharaoh to let My people go free." Soon Moses was on his way to Egypt to do what God said.

God speaks to us through the Bible, other people, and things that happen.
Moses heard God in a burning bush.

I will listen to God's voice and obey Him.

The Red Sea

—I FEEL LIKE TRAVELIN' ON—

"The Lord has been so good to me, I feel like travelin' on."

from
EXODUS 14

Pharaoh let God's people go free. But then he changed his mind and sent his army to capture them. God's people saw Pharaoh's army coming. They were frightened! They had no way of escape. Pharaoh's army was behind them. The sea was before them. But Moses trusted God. He shouted, "Do not be afraid! God will save you!" Then Moses lifted his staff and the Red Sea parted. God made a road through the middle of the sea! As they reached the other side, God let the water go back and the army could not go through it. God's people were saved!

God can make a way when there is no way.
God parted the Red Sea for
Moses and God's people.

I will trust God to make a way for me!

The Ten Commandments

"God's Word is wonderful, keeping us from harm".

from
EXODUS 20

Moses led the Israelites through the desert. On the way, God told Moses to go to Mount Sinai. There He gave Moses ten important rules to follow. God wrote the Ten Commandments on stone tablets. A commandment is not something you *might* do. It is something you *must* do. God said these ten rules were to be obeyed. God knew that if the people obeyed the Ten Commandments they would live safe and happy lives.

God's ways are true.

God gave us the Ten Commandments
as rules to follow.

I will honor God. I will obey His rules.

Balaam & the Talking Donkey

—ANGELS WATCHIN' OVER ME—

"All night, all day, angels watchin' over me."

from NUMBERS 22

Balaam made a poor choice. A bad king had offered Balaam a lot of money if he would say unkind things about the people of God. He took the money and left on his donkey to serve the bad king. God was not pleased with Balaam. He sent an angel with a flaming sword to block his way. Balaam didn't see the angel in the road but his donkey did. Three times, the donkey ran off the road. Three times, Balaam beat his donkey. God made the donkey speak, "Why do you hit me?" Balaam couldn't believe it— a talking donkey! Then Balaam saw the angel too. He told God he was sorry. God forgave him, and Balaam returned to bless God's people.

God sends helpers to show us His way.
Balaam listened and followed God's direction.

I will listen to people who teach me God's way.

Promised Land

*"O when the saints go marching in,
Lord I want to be in that number."*

from
DEUTERONOMY 34

Moses and the Israelites had traveled in the desert for forty years. God taught them many things. He taught them to trust Him. He taught them to obey. He showed them His power. After years of learning God's lessons, they were ready to enter the Promised Land. Moses did not get to go, but he watched from Mount Nebo. He was happy as he watched the people of God march into the Promised Land. It was a great day!

God blesses those who learn His lessons.
The Israelites were blessed.

I will learn God's lessons and look forward to His blessings.

Rahab's Hidden Secret

—I'M IN THE LORD'S ARMY—

"I may never...ride in the calvary...but I'm in the Lord's army!"

from JOSHUA 2

Joshua was a brave soldier. He sent two spies into Jericho to find out how his army could defeat the enemy. The spies went to Rahab's house. Rahab had heard about God's power. She wanted to help these men because she knew God was on their side. The king of Jericho found out that the two spies were in the city. He sent his soldiers to find them. Rahab hid the two spies to help them escape. The soldiers came looking... looking... looking, but they did not find the spies. Because Rahab helped the men, God protected her and her family.

Soldiers in God's army help each other.
Rahab helped the spies and was saved.

I will help God's people.

Joshua's Battle of Jericho

—JOSHUA FIT THE BATTLE OF JERICHO—

"Joshua fit the battle of Jericho, and the walls came tumbling down."

from JOSHUA 6

The two spies returned to Joshua. They told him that the people of Jericho were afraid. A very tall wall surrounded Jericho. The wall was made of stone. How would they ever get through the wall? God told Joshua and his army to march around Jericho each day for six days. On the seventh day, the people were to march around the city seven times. They blew the trumpets and shouted really loud! When Joshua obeyed God, the walls of Jericho came tumbling down! God's way won the battle.

God's ways are not our ways.

Joshua fought the battle of Jericho
God's way and won.

I will do things God's way.

Samson

"God is our refuge and strength,
an ever present help in trouble."

from
JUDGES 16

Samson was in big trouble! Once he was the strongest man in the world. No one could defeat him. God had given him a mighty strength. But now it was gone. As long as Samson obeyed God, his strength remained. But he had not obeyed. So there he stood, tied between two pillars in the enemy's temple. But Samson prayed, "Lord give me strength one more time." Then Samson pushed the pillars down, making the temple roof fall down on the enemy. God answered Samson's prayers and saved His people.

God will give us the strength we need when we ask Him.

Samson prayed for strength and God supplied it.

I will pray for strength in the Lord.

Ruth

—THIS IS MY COMMANDMENT—

"This is my commandment, that you love one another."

from RUTH

Naomi, her husband, and their two sons moved to a far away land. Her sons married women named Orpah and Ruth. But Naomi's husband and sons died. Naomi was very sad. She wanted to go home. Naomi told Orpah and Ruth they could go home to their mothers. Orpah did that. But Ruth loved Naomi and could not leave her. She told Naomi, "Where you go, I will go. Your people will be my people, and your God, my God." So Ruth went with Naomi. Because of her kindness, God blessed Ruth with a husband and children.

God blesses us when we are kind and love one another.

Ruth showed love and kindness to Naomi.

I will show love and kindness to others.

Hannah's Prayer

—DO LORD—

"Do Lord, oh do Lord, oh do remember me."

from
1 SAMUEL 1

Hannah was very sad because she had no children. One day, Hannah and her husband went to the temple. Hannah prayed, "Lord, remember me. If You will give me a son, I will give him back to You. When he is old enough, I will bring him back to this temple to serve You." God heard Hannah's prayer and gave her a baby boy. She named him Samuel. Hannah kept her promise to God. When Samuel was old enough, Hannah brought him to the temple. Samuel served the Lord his whole life.

God answers our prayers.

God remembered Hannah's prayers
and gave her a son.

When I pray, I know God hears me.

Young Samuel

—THE LORD IS MY HELPER—

"The Lord is my helper."

from
1 SAMUEL 3

When Samuel was a young boy, he became God's helper. Young Samuel lived in the temple with Eli, the prophet. One night, Samuel heard a voice call him. He thought it was Eli. Samuel got up and went to Eli. "Here I am," he said. Eli told Samuel he hadn't called him. Samuel went back to bed. Again, Samuel heard the voice. Eli told Samuel if he heard the voice calling again to say, "Speak, Lord. I am listening." Soon Samuel heard the voice. This time Samuel answered, "Speak, Lord. I am listening." And God spoke to Samuel. Samuel listened and grew up to be one of God's best helpers.

It is good to listen to God and be His helper.
Samuel was God's helper and heard His voice.

I will listen and be God's helper too!

David Sings Praises

—LITTLE DAVID, PLAY ON YOUR HARP—

"Little David, play on your harp. Hallelu, hallelu!"

from
1 SAMUEL 16:14-23

Saul was the king of Israel. Sometimes Saul would become very sad and grumpy. One of Saul's servants thought that listening to happy music would make Saul feel better. He knew a shepherd boy named David who could sing praise songs and play the harp. David loved to praise God with his music. So the servant sent for David. David came to the palace and played his harp and sang for the king. The king felt much better. Singing songs about the Lord pleases God and can make anyone feel better!

God is worthy of praise.

David sang praise songs to make Saul feel better.

I will sing songs of praise!

David Fights Goliath

—ONLY A BOY NAMED DAVID—

"Only a boy named David, only a little sling."

from
1 SAMUEL 17

The Philistine army came to fight God's people. The Philistines had a giant warrior named Goliath. Goliath was over nine feet tall. He wore a suit of armor and carried a heavy spear. Every morning, the giant shouted mean words and made fun of God. God's people were afraid. But David the shepherd boy said, "I'll fight that giant!" David took his slingshot and found five stones. David shouted to Goliath, "You come with a sword and a spear! But I come in the name of God!" David put one stone in his slingshot. Whizzzz! The stone hit Goliath in the forehead. He fell like a big tree. David won! God was on his side.

If God is on our side we can do great things.

With God's help, David won the
battle against Goliath.

I will call on the Lord and He will help me.

David and Jonathan

"Sharing is really caring, caring about the friends you know."

from
1 SAMUEL 18:1-4

David went to live in the king's house. There he met Jonathan, the king's son. Jonathan and David became best friends. Jonathan gave David a present. He gave David his own coat. He also gave David his sword, bow, arrow, and belt. They made a special promise to each other. "We will always be friends. We will always help each other." God had a wonderful plan for David's life. God's blessings were on David. Soon he would become a great king and mighty soldier.

Sharing pleases God.
Jonathan showed David his
friendship by sharing.

I will share with my friends.

David and Mephibosheth

—KINDNESS—

"Be kind, every day. Be kind in every way."

from
2 SAMUEL 9

King Saul and his son Jonathan were both killed in battle. God chose David as the new king. In those days, the children of the old king were usually sent away. But David was a kind king. He sent for Jonathan's crippled son, Mephibosheth. Mephibosheth was afraid. But David said, "Don't be afraid. I loved your father Jonathan. You are welcome in my house. Please come and eat dinner with me." Because of David's kindness, Mephibosheth became part of the king's family.

God said to be kind to one another.
David was kind to Mephibosheth.

I will show kindness to others.

Elijah's Victory

— CLIMB SUNSHINE MOUNTAIN —

"Climb, climb up Sunshine Mountain, faces all aglow."

from
1 KINGS 18

Bad King Ahab and his wife did not love God. They served a false god named Baal. One day the prophet Elijah told King Ahab to meet him on Mount Carmel. Then Elijah spoke. "Let's find out who is the true God." They agreed to build an altar and lay wood upon it. The god who sends fire from heaven will be the one true god. All day, Ahab's prophets prayed to their false god Baal. Nothing happened. Then Elijah poured water all over his altar and then called to God, "Today, O Lord, let it be known that You are the one true God!" Instantly fire fell from heaven. Everyone knew Elijah's God was the one true God.

There is only one true God.

Elijah told people about the one true God.

I will tell people about the one true God.

Elijah's Chariot of Fire

—SWING LOW, SWEET CHARIOT—

"Swing low, sweet chariot, comin' for to carry me home."

from 2 KINGS 2:9-12

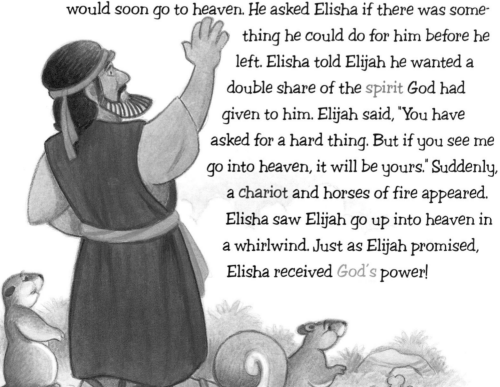

The preacher Elijah served God for many years. When Elijah was old, he needed a helper. He chose Elisha. Elisha loved God too. Elijah knew he would soon go to heaven. He asked Elisha if there was something he could do for him before he left. Elisha told Elijah he wanted a double share of the spirit God had given to him. Elijah said, "You have asked for a hard thing. But if you see me go into heaven, it will be yours." Suddenly, a chariot and horses of fire appeared. Elisha saw Elijah go up into heaven in a whirlwind. Just as Elijah promised, Elisha received God's power!

God has prepared a home in heaven for those who serve Him.

Elijah was taken to heaven in a fiery chariot.

God has a home in heaven for me.

Naaman

—TO OBEY IS BETTER—

"To obey is better than sacrifice."

from
2 KINGS 5:1-14

Naaman commanded the king's army. He was a very important man. But he was also a very sick man. He had sores all over his body. One day, Naaman heard about a man named Elisha. Elisha had done many wonderful things. Naaman sent his servant to ask Elisha how to get well. Elisha prayed and God told him exactly what to do. Elisha told the servant to tell Naaman to go to the Jordan River and wash seven times. Six times wouldn't do. So Naaman went down into the water seven times. The sores were gone! God made Naaman well!

We should trust God and follow His instructions.

Naaman did exactly as God said and he was healed.

I will do exactly what God says.

Nehemiah's Wall

—BUILDING OTHERS UP—

"Building, building, building others up,
with a kind word or a compliment."

from
NEHEMIAH 1-2

Nehemiah was a servant of the king. One day, Nehemiah's brother came from their homeland with sad news. The walls of Jerusalem, where they used to live, were falling down. This made Nehemiah very sad. Nehemiah didn't know how to get the wall rebuilt. So he did the only thing he knew to do. He prayed. He asked God to help his people. The king noticed Nehemiah's sad face. He asked, "Why are you so sad?" Nehemiah told him about the broken-down wall. The king said a kind word, "Go and help your people rebuild the wall. Come back when it is finished." Nehemiah thanked God for answering his prayer.

When you don't know what to do, pray.
Nehemiah prayed for help, and God helped him.

When I don't know what to do, I will pray.

Queen Esther

"For such a time as this...God brought us here."

from
ESTHER

Esther, a beautiful Jewish girl, married a king. Esther's cousin Mordecai was the king's good helper. Haman was also a helper, but he was bad. Haman didn't like the Jews. He had a plan to kill Mordecai and all the Jews. Mordecai heard about Haman's plan and told Esther, "Perhaps God has made you queen for such a time as this." Queen Esther asked the king to save her and her people.

Then Esther told the king about Haman's evil plan to kill all the Jews. The king was angry with Haman. Because of Esther, God's people were saved!

You were born at just the right time.

Esther was born at just the right time to serve God.

I was born at the right time to serve God.

Job

—GOD IS SO GOOD—

"God is so good, He's so good to me."

from
JOB

Job was a good man and a blessing to others. God blessed him with a wonderful family, wealth, and good health. Every morning, Job thanked God for his many blessings. One day, Job lost all he owned. Then Job's children were killed in a great storm. But Job still trusted God. He said, "The Lord gives; and the Lord takes away. Praise the name of the Lord!" Then Job became very sick. Job did not blame God for his sickness. Job knew there are some things we cannot understand. God was pleased with Job and healed him. And He gave Job more children, crops, and animals!

We should praise the Lord in good times and bad.
Job praised the Lord, even in bad times.

I will praise the Lord all the time!

Ezekiel's Wheel

—EZEKIEL'S WHEEL—

"Ezekiel saw a wheel, way up in the middle of the air."

from
EZEKIEL 1

Prophet Ezekiel had a dream as he looked up into the sky. He saw a stormy wind with lightning flashes and very bright lights. He saw four angels with wings. Beside each angel was a sparkling wheel. Each wheel had a smaller wheel spinning inside it. Above the angels were a beautiful throne and a dazzling rainbow. On the throne was a figure like a man. Ezekiel's dream was about God. How mighty our God is! He is not like us. He is God! Ezekiel bowed down to show God honor and respect.

God is greater than we are.
Ezekiel bowed down to honor God.

I will honor and respect God.

Ezekiel's Dry Bones

—DRY BONES—

"Dem bones, dem bones, dem dry bones, now hear the word of the Lord."

from EZEKIEL 37:1-14

One night Ezekiel had another strange dream. He dreamed he was taken to the middle of a large valley full of old, dry bones. God asked Ezekiel, "Can these bones live?" Ezekiel answered, "I don't know, Lord. Only You know that!" Ezekiel watched as the dry bones stood up and became an army. Then God explained the dream. "My people are sad. They think things will not get better. Tell them that things will get better. They will return to the Promised Land." Ezekiel told the people what God said. "Dry bones can live. All things are possible with God!"

All things are possible with God.

Ezekiel believed that God could do anything.

I believe God can do all things!

Shadrach, Meshach, and Abednego

—HIS BANNER OVER ME IS LOVE—

"The Lord is mine and I am His, His banner over me is love."

from
DANIEL 3

A bad king made a golden statue. He made everyone bow down before the statue when the music played. "If you don't bow down," he said, "I will throw you into the fire." Everyone bowed except Shadrach, Meshach, and Abednego. They would not bow down to a statue. They would only bow down to God. The king had the men thrown into the hot fire. The king was amazed. "Didn't I throw three men into the fire?" he asked. "I see four men walking around!" He called the men to come out of the fire. They were not even burned! The king believed in God and praised Him.

When we are afraid we can trust in God.

Shadrach, Meshach, and Abednego trusted God,
even when they were afraid.

I will trust God even when I am afraid.

Daniel in the Lion's Den

—WHISPER A PRAYER—

"God answers prayer in the morning, God answers prayer at noon."

from
DANIEL 6

Daniel loved God and prayed to Him every day. The king put Daniel in charge of the whole kingdom. This made the other leaders jealous. They wanted to get rid of Daniel. So they came up with an evil plan. They made a law that said it was wrong to pray. But Daniel was a good man. He kept praying. The bad men took Daniel to the king. "Daniel broke the law! Throw him to the lions!" Daniel was dropped into a pit full of hungry lions. But God sent an angel to shut the lions' mouths. God saved Daniel!

God answers our prayers when we are in trouble.

Daniel prayed when he needed help.

I will pray when I need help.

Jonah Runs away from God

—JONAH'S SONG—

"Sailor, sailor, sailor afraid, call upon the Lord in your trouble."

from JONAH 1:1-15

God told Jonah to go to Ninevah and tell the people there about God's love. Jonah didn't want to go. He tried to run away from God on a ship. But you can't hide from God. God caused a big storm. The sailors were afraid, but Jonah was fast asleep. They woke Jonah. "Pray to your God. Ask Him to save us." Jonah knew the storm was his fault. Then Jonah said a strange thing: "Throw me overboard and the storm will stop." They threw Jonah into the water, and down he sank.

God has a job for everyone.
God had a job for Jonah.

I will do the job that God has for me.

Jonah and the Big Fish

—WHO DID SWALLOW JONAH?—

"Who did, who did, who did swallow Jonah?"

from
JONAH 1:17 — 3:10

As Jonah sank beneath the waves, he was swallowed by a big fish. Jonah was in the stomach of that fish for three days and three nights! He was sorry he had disobeyed. He prayed and prayed. He asked God to forgive him for running away. God's love is so wonderful. God forgave Jonah. So God told the big fish to spit Jonah up on the seashore. Then Jonah obeyed God. He got up and went to Ninevah. He told the people to stop doing bad things. The people told God they were sorry. They were saved because Jonah obeyed!

God is a forgiving God.

He forgave Jonah even though he disobeyed.

I know God will forgive me if I say I'm sorry.

David's Shepherd

—THE LORD IS MY SHEPHERD—

"The Lord is my shepherd, I shall not be in want."

from PSALM 23

When you have to make a big decision, to whom do you turn? When you don't know which way to go, whom do you ask? When you need protection from life's many dangers, where do you go? David went to his Shepherd. Who is that, you ask? "The Lord is my Shepherd," David wrote. "He leads me. He protects me. He restores me." And like sheep, we will follow Him.

We can trust God to lead and protect us.

David followed God like sheep follow a shepherd.

I will follow God and know He'll protect me.

94

David's Fears

—WHEN I AM AFRAID—

"When I am afraid, I will trust in You, my Father."

from
PSALM 56

David was very brave. He had marched down into a valley to fight a giant named Goliath. He had led great armies into battle and won the victory. But in Psalm 56 we see another side of David. We see David alone and afraid. His enemies are calling him names and doing bad things. David's eyes are full of tears as he cries out to God, "When I am afraid, I will trust in You." David knew that God could help him. God is bigger than any fear!

God can calm our biggest fears.

David trusted God when he was afraid.

I will trust God to help me when I'm afraid.

David Praised the Lord

—PRAISE THE LORD TOGETHER—

"Come praise the Lord together, singing, 'Alleluia, 'Alleluia, 'Alleluia,'"

from
PSALMS 71; 148; 150

David wrote in the book of Psalms, "It is good to praise the Lord. "When we praise the Lord we tell Him how good and wonderful we think He is. When we praise God, we let Him know how much we love Him. David praised the Lord with the harp. He praised Him with singing and dancing. He praised Him first thing in the morning. Then he praised Him in the evening when the sun went down. And do you know what? We can too!

It is good to praise the Lord!
David praised the Lord all the time.

I will praise the Lord and tell Him I love Him.

God's Great Big World

"This is my Father's world, and to my listening ears, all nature sings."

from
PSALMS 136

When David was a shepherd boy, he spent many nights alone. On the hillside it was quiet, so David wrote lots of songs. In Psalm 136, David wrote, "God made the heavens. He made every star that shines. God made the earth. He made everything that lives on the earth. And God made the skies and the sea." God shows His love for us in nature all around us. This truly is our Father's world!

Praise God because He made our world.
David praised God for making
the heavens and the earth.

I see all God made and I praise Him.

As Wise As an Owl

—APPLY—

"Apply your heart to instruction and your ears to the words of knowledge."

from PROVERBS 23:12

You've heard the saying "wise old owl." Do you know who was the wisest man who ever lived? The Bible says there was no one wiser than Solomon. What were some of the things this wise man did? First, he knew God's Word. Then he applied God's Word in his life. To apply means to put into practice. How can you be wise like Solomon? Know God's Word and apply what the Bible says!

It is wise to put God's Word into practice.

Solomon was wise to apply God's Word.

I will read my Bible and do what it teaches.

New Testament

Gabriel Visits Mary

—FAIREST LORD JESUS—

"Fairest Lord Jesus, Ruler of all nature,
O Thou of God and man the Son."

from
LUKE 1:26-38

A young woman named Mary loved God with all her heart. One day an angel named Gabriel came to visit Mary. He had a message from God. When Mary saw the angel she was afraid. But the angel said, "Do not be afraid. God is pleased with you. He is going to give you a special baby. The baby will be God's own Son. You will name Him Jesus." Mary was amazed. She asked the angel, "How can this be true?" The angel answered, "Nothing is impossible with God!" Mary believed and thanked God.

Nothing is impossible with God.
Mary believed God could do anything.

I believe God can do anything too!

The Savior Is Born

—AWAY IN A MANGER—

"Away in a manger, no crib for a bed, the little Lord Jesus laid down His sweet head.

from
LUKE 2:1-14

Clip, clop, clip, clop. Mary rode on the donkey back to Bethlehem. "Joseph," she said, "it's time for my baby to be born!" Joseph looked for a place to stay. But the answer was always the same: "We have no room." Joseph found a stable full of cows and sheep. There they could stay. On that special night the baby Jesus was born. Mary wrapped Jesus in cloth and laid Him in a manger, a feeding box full of hay. The animals must have been very surprised! That night angels sang and praised God: "Glory to God in the highest and peace on earth!" Jesus, God's Son, was born!

God always takes care of our needs.
He gave baby Jesus a bed.

I will trust God to take care of me.

Wise Men Come

—BEHOLD THAT STAR—

"Behold that star, it is the star of Bethlehem."

from
MATTHEW 2:1-12

The three wise men had seen a lot of stars. But they had never seen a special star like this one! This star was moving across the eastern sky. And night after night they followed it. They knew God was using it to guide them to a new king. The journey was long. But finally the star stopped and came to rest over Bethlehem. Beneath the star they found the baby Jesus. When they saw Him they bowed down and worshiped Him. They gave Jesus gifts of gold, frankincense, and myrrh. They knew Jesus was Lord.

God guides us to Jesus so we can worship Him.
Wise men followed the star to worship Jesus.

I will worship Jesus.

Jesus in the Temple

—WE'RE GOING TO GOD'S HOUSE TODAY—

*"Wake up sleepy head, open your eyes...
we're going to God's house today."*

from
LUKE 2:41-52

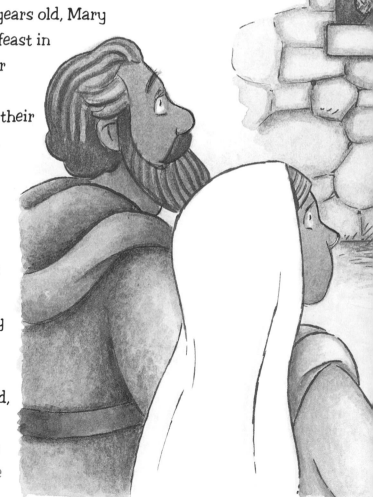

When Jesus was twelve years old, Mary and Joseph took Him to a feast in Jerusalem. They walked for several days to get there. It was fun traveling with their friends. On the way home, Mary and Joseph realized Jesus wasn't with them. They couldn't find Him among their family or friends. They hurried back to Jerusalem. They looked for three days! Finally they found Jesus in the temple. Mary said, "Jesus, where have you been?" Jesus said, "Didn't you know I'd be in My Father's house?" Jesus loved to go to God's house and talk about God.

106

It is good to learn about God.
Jesus loved to go to the temple and talk about God.

I like to go to church and learn about God.

John Baptizes Jesus

—DOWN BY THE RIVERSIDE—

"Gonna lay down my burden, down by the riverside."

from
MATTHEW 3:13-17;
MARK 1:9-11; LUKE 3:21-22;
JOHN 1:29-33

John the Baptist lived in the desert. He ate wild honey and locusts. John told people about God. Jesus said that John was a great man. One day while John was baptizing believers, Jesus came to him. He walked right into the Jordan River and said to John, "Baptize Me." John knew Jesus was God's Son. He said, "You should be the one baptizing me." But John did as Jesus asked. Down in the water Jesus went. When He came up, the Spirit of God came and landed on His shoulder. It looked like a dove. God said, "This is My Son and I love Him."

Baptism shows the world that we love Jesus.
Jesus was baptized and pleased God.

When I am baptized, God will be pleased.

Jesus Calls His Disciples

—I HAVE DECIDED TO FOLLOW JESUS—

"I have decided to follow Jesus."

from
MATTHEW 4:18-22;
MARK 1:16-20; LUKE 5:1-11;
JOHN 1:35-42

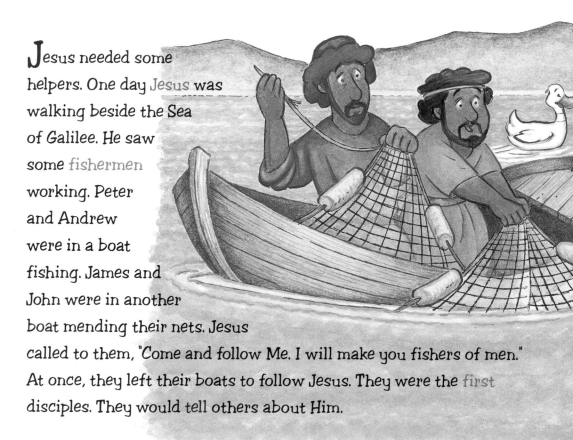

Jesus needed some helpers. One day Jesus was walking beside the Sea of Galilee. He saw some fishermen working. Peter and Andrew were in a boat fishing. James and John were in another boat mending their nets. Jesus called to them, "Come and follow Me. I will make you fishers of men." At once, they left their boats to follow Jesus. They were the first disciples. They would tell others about Him.

Jesus calls us to be His disciples.
Peter and Andrew left their
nets and followed Jesus.

I will follow Jesus and tell others about Him.

The Beatitudes

—THE BEATITUDES—

"Blessed are the pure in heart. They will see God."

from
MATTHEW 5:1-12;
LUKE 6:20-26

Many people came to hear Jesus teach. One day, the crowd was so big Jesus had to go up on a mountainside. Once there, He told everyone about the Beatitudes. He said, "People who are sad now will be happy. And people who are kind will be shown kindness. The pure will see God. God will satisfy those who want to know Him more. And those who are treated badly because they do good things will be happy. Be glad. We have great rewards waiting in heaven!"

Following Jesus makes us happy.
Many people follow Jesus.

I will follow Jesus too.

Shine for Jesus

—JESUS WANTS ME FOR A SUNBEAM—

"A sunbeam, a sunbeam, Jesus wants me for a sunbeam."

from
MATTHEW 5:14-16

Every morning the bright yellow sun comes up. As the sun begins to shine, the darkness goes away. Jesus said that we should be like the sunbeams. We are to bring light to a dark world. When we tell the truth, we bring light to the world. When we are kind, we bring light to the world. When we tell our friends about God's love, we bring light to the world. Yes, Jesus wants us to shine, just like a sunbeam!

Jesus' followers do good things to honor Him.

Jesus said we are a light to the
world when we do good things for Him.

I will shine for Jesus.

Pray Like Jesus

—JESUS IN THE MORNING—

"Jesus in the morning, Jesus at the noontide... Jesus when the sun goes down."

from
LUKE 11:2-4

Praying is talking with God. Jesus prayed every day. He taught His followers how to pray. He was a good example. Jesus said we should find a quiet place where we can be alone with God. Early in the morning, while it was still dark, Jesus got up. He left the house and went to a place to be alone with God. There He talked to His heavenly Father. Jesus also talked to His heavenly Father in the morning, afternoon, evening—all the time! We can talk to God too, just like Jesus!

Pray all the time.

Jesus taught that anytime is the right time to pray.

I can pray anytime.

Do Not Judge

—DO NOT JUDGE—

"Do not judge, or you too will be judged."

from
MATTHEW 7:1-5;
LUKE 6:37-42

Jesus doesn't want us to judge another person's actions. When we judge, we decide if someone is doing good or bad. That's not our job; it's God's job. God wants us to make right choices and look at our own lives. Jesus said, "Do not judge others. If you do, you too will be judged. In the same way you judge others, you will be judged." If we're harsh and unkind, we will be judged the very same way. Before we tell others about something they are doing wrong, we must stop doing wrong ourselves.

We should not judge others.
Jesus said, "Do not judge."

I will not judge what others do.

Ask, Seek, and Knock

—ASK, SEEK, AND KNOCK—

"Ask and it will be given to you, seek and you will find."

Jesus taught His disciples that they should never stop praying. He said, "Keep asking in prayer, and it will be given to you. Keep seeking, and you will find what you are looking for. Keep knocking and the door will open!" God always hears our prayers and He will answer! So never quit praying!

God has promised to answer our prayers.
Jesus said to ask God for what you need.

I know God hears and answers my prayers.

The Golden Rule

—DO TO OTHERS—

"Do, do, do, do, do, do, do, do to others."

from
MATTHEW 7:12

Jesus taught His twelve disciples a very important lesson. He said we should always treat others the way we want to be treated. It's called the Golden Rule. It's golden because it's the most valuable lesson we can ever learn. It's called a rule because we need to do this all the time, not just some of the time. If you want to be treated kindly, treat others with kindness. If you want to be loved, show love to others. If we obey this rule, we will be happy and God will be pleased.

Show kindness to everyone.

Jesus said to treat other people the way you want to be treated.

I will show kindness and obey the Golden Rule.

The Wise Man Built His House

—THE WISE MAN BUILT HIS HOUSE UPON THE ROCK—

"The wise man built his house upon the rock."

from
MATTHEW 7:24-29;
LUKE 6:47-49

Jesus said there are wise people and foolish people. He said a wise person is like a builder who builds his house upon a rock. Rocks are strong and do not wash away. So a house built on a rock will stand. The Bible is like a solid rock. It is God's Word to us. If we do the things the Bible says to do, we will be strong. Wise people read the Bible and do what it says. When we build our lives on the solid rock of God's Word, we will stand strong for Jesus!

Wise people do what the Bible says.

Jesus taught about wise and foolish people.

I will do what the Bible says.

A Hole in the Roof

—KUMBAYA—

"Kumbaya, my Lord, kumbaya."

from
MATTHEW 9:1-8;
MARK 2:1-12; LUKE 5:17-25

Jesus was teaching inside a house full of people. They were even standing outside, looking through the windows and doors! Four men arrived. They were carrying their friend, who could not walk. They wanted Jesus to heal him. When they couldn't get through the crowd, they had an idea. They carried their friend on his mat up onto the roof. They made a hole in the roof and lowered their friend down. Jesus told the man to pick up his mat and go home. The man stood up! His friends were glad and all the people praised God!

Jesus can help our friends.

Four men brought their friend to Jesus.

I will bring my friends to Jesus.

Jesus Calms the Storm

—WHAT A MIGHTY HAND—

"What a mighty hand, a mighty hand has He."

from
MATTHEW 8:23-27;
MARK 4:35-41;
LUKE 8:22-25

One day, Jesus and His disciples were sailing across a lake. He was very tired from teaching all day. So a sleepy Jesus took a nap in the back of the boat. While He was sleeping, there came a terrible storm. The waves crashed against the boat. The disciples woke Jesus up saying, "Teacher, don't you care if we drown?" Jesus got up, faced the wind, and shouted to the storm, "Quiet! Be still!" At His word, the wind stopped and the waters were calmed. The disciples were amazed. They said, "Even the wind and waves obey Him!"

God is in control.

Jesus controls the wind and the sea.

I won't be afraid. God is in control.

Jesus Heals

—WHAT A FRIEND WE HAVE IN JESUS—

"What a friend we have in Jesus, All our sins and griefs to bear."

from
MATTHEW 9:20-22;
MARK 5:25-34;
LUKE 8:43-48

Everywhere Jesus went there were crowds of people. Some people came to hear Him teach. Some needed His help. One woman in the crowd wanted Jesus to make her well. She thought, "If I could just get close enough to touch His clothes, I'm sure I would get well!" She pushed through the crowd until she got close to Jesus. She stretched out her hand and touched the edge of His coat. As soon as she touched Him, she was well! Jesus asked, "Who touched Me?" The woman thanked Jesus for making her well.

Jesus can heal everyone.
He made a sick woman well.

When I am sick, I will ask Jesus to help me.

Parable of the Pearl

—HAPPY ALL THE TIME—

"I'm in right, outright, upright, downright, happy all the time."

from
MATTHEW 13:45-46

Jesus said the kingdom of heaven is like a pearl. Once a man found a pearl worth lots of money. It was the most beautiful pearl in all the world. To get it, he would have to sell everything he had. But it was worth it! Heaven is like that. There is no treasure on earth that compares to heaven. It is better than anything in this world. It is worth everything you have to get it. Earthly things don't last long, but heaven is forever!

Heaven is more wonderful than anything on earth.
We should let nothing on earth
keep us from heaven.

I will thank God for making heaven for me!

Parable of the Net

—I WILL MAKE YOU FISHERS OF MEN—

"I will make you fishers of men, if you follow Me."

from
MATTHEW 13:47-50

Once Jesus told a story about a fisherman. This fisherman threw his net out into the lake. Many fish swam into the net. The fisherman waited until the net was full. Then he pulled the net in. He began to sort the good fish from the bad fish. Jesus explained, "Heaven is like the fisherman's net. Everyone wants to go to heaven. But one day the angels will sort out the people who really love God from the people who don't. The people who really love God will go to heaven. But those who do not love God will not."

All Christians will go to heaven.
Heaven is a wonderful place.

I love God. I will go to heaven!

Jesus Loves You

"For God so loved the world, He gave His only Son."

from
JOHN 3:16

In the Bible, we find a wonderful promise. John 3:16 says that God loves you and me. He loves your mom and dad. He loves everyone in your family. He loves all your neighbors. In fact, He loves everyone in your city and state. Yes, His love is so big that it reaches out to everyone in the whole world. And God did something to prove it. He gave His only Son, Jesus, to save everyone who believes in Him. Now all these people can live in heaven forever if they trust Jesus. What a wonderful promise!

God loved us so much, He sent His Son!
Jesus came to save us.

I thank God for sending Jesus!

Pool at Bethesda

—ROLL AWAY—

"Roll away, roll away, roll away.
All the burdens of my heart roll away."

from
JOHN 5:1-8

Bethesda was a very special pool. Every day sick and hurting people went there. The water of Bethesda was usually calm. But sometimes an angel would come and stir the water. When the water stirred, the first person into the pool would be healed. One day Jesus saw a man who couldn't walk sitting by the pool. Jesus asked him, "Don't you want to get well?" The man said, "Yes, but I have no one to help me get into the pool." Then Jesus said, "Pick up your mat and walk." The man obeyed and was healed. He stood up and walked away happy!

Jesus has the power to heal.
He healed the crippled man.

I know Jesus can make sick people well.

Feeding of 5,000

—GIVE THANKS TO THE LORD—

"O give thanks to the Lord, for He is good, He is good."

from
MATTHEW 14:13-21;
MARK 6:35-43;
LUKE 9:11-17

People came from near and far to hear Jesus teach. One day many people gathered to listen. After a while the people were hungry. Jesus asked His disciples to feed them. They said, "We don't have enough money to feed them, but here is a boy who has five loaves of bread and two fish. He is willing to share." Jesus took the boy's lunch, looked up to heaven, and gave thanks. He began breaking the bread and fish into pieces. It fed over five thousand people and there were twelve basketfuls left! A little bit goes a long way in Jesus' hands.

Give what you have to Jesus and He will bless it.
A little boy shared his lunch with a crowd.

I will share what I have.

Jesus Walks on Water

—FOOTPRINTS ON THE WATER—

"I saw footprints on the water, footprints on the sea."

from
MATTHEW 14:22-32;
MARK 6:45-51

One evening the disciples were rowing their boat across the lake. Suddenly, a mighty wind blew. It caused their boat to be tossed back and forth on the waves. Jesus saw they were in trouble. He went out to them, walking on the water! When the disciples saw Jesus walking on the lake, they thought He was a ghost. They were afraid. Jesus called to them, "Don't be afraid!" As He climbed into the boat, the wind calmed down. The disciples were amazed. They said, "Truly You are the Son of God!"

Jesus can do anything.

He even walked on water.

I am not afraid. Jesus can do anything.

Faith Is Like a Mustard Seed

—THE MUSTARD SEED—

from
MATTHEW 17:20;
LUKE 17:6

"If you have faith as small as a mustard seed... nothing will be impossible for you."

A giant oak tree wasn't always so big. It started out as a little seed. Big things usually start out small. Jesus once explained that faith in God works that way. He said our faith is like a tiny little mustard seed. Farmers plant them in gardens. The sun and rain help the seed grow strong and tall. When we start loving God, we love just a little. But as we grow, God helps us love more and more. Our faith grows more and more, just like a little mustard seed. Jesus said that as our faith grows, nothing will be impossible for us!

Faith starts small and grows big.
It's just like a mustard seed.

I believe that my faith will grow and grow!

Fishing for Gold

—GO FISH, GO FISH—

"Go fish, go fish, fishin' for the Lord."

from
MATTHEW 17:24-27

Peter was worried. Jesus didn't have any money to pay the tax collector. Peter didn't have any money either. But Jesus wasn't worried. He knew God would take care of them. But how? Jesus told Peter to go fishing. When he caught his first fish, he was to look in the fish's mouth. Peter didn't understand, but he did as Jesus said. When Peter caught his first fish, he looked in the fish's mouth. There he found a gold coin! Now there was plenty of money to pay the taxes. God had given them what they needed.

God will take care of our needs.
He met the disciples needs.

I will trust God to take care of me.

Throw the First Stone

—JESUS LOVES ME—

"Jesus loves me, this I know, for the Bible tells me so."

from
JOHN 8:1-11

The Bible says that one day Jesus was teaching the people in the temple. A woman was brought before Him. She had done a very bad thing. The people were going to throw stones at her. Jesus wanted to show the people how to love one another. He said, "If you've never done anything wrong, throw the first stone." Everyone walked away. Jesus showed them how to love.

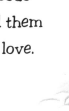

We should love one another.
Jesus loved and cared for sinners.

Jesus loves me, and I will love others.

A Blind Man Sees

—REJOICE IN THE LORD ALWAYS—

"Rejoice in the Lord always, and again I say, rejoice!"

from
JOHN 9:1-7

*O*nce there was a man who was born blind. He could not see the blue sky or the sunshine. He could not see the faces of the people who loved him. Jesus wanted to help this man. He did something strange. Jesus spit on the ground and made some mud. He put the mud on the blind man's eyes. Then Jesus told him to go and wash. The blind man obeyed. As the mud washed from his eyes, he saw the blue sky. He saw the sunshine. He was blind, but now he could see!

Jesus has the power to heal.
He healed a blind man.

I will praise Jesus for His healing power.

Jesus, the Good Shepherd

—I AM THE GOOD SHEPHERD—

"And the good shepherd lays down his life for the sheep."

from JOHN 10:11-14

Jesus once said that people are like sheep. And He is like a good shepherd. Sheep aren't very smart. They don't know which way to go. They get lost. That's why they must listen for the shepherd's voice. They must follow him. Sheep never follow a stranger's voice. In fact, they run away from strangers. Jesus said, "I am the Good Shepherd, and I am ready to protect My sheep." Jesus loves you and will take care of you!

Jesus is the Good Shepherd.

He loves and protects His sheep.

I know Jesus loves me and will take care of me.

The Good Samaritan

"Love your neighbor as yourself...We gotta show a little kindness."

from
LUKE 10:25-37

A teacher of the law asked Jesus, "You said we are to love our neighbor as ourselves. Who is our neighbor?" Jesus answered with a story. "A man was traveling to Jericho. Robbers beat him and took everything. A priest came along, but he passed by on the other side of the road. A temple worker also passed by without stopping to help. But when a man from Samaria saw the hurt man, he stopped and helped him!" Then Jesus said, "Which one was a good neighbor?" The teacher answered, "The one who treated him kindly." Then Jesus said, "Go and do the same thing!"

We are to love our neighbor as ourselves.

Jesus says that we should be like the Good Samaritan.

I will be a good neighbor and help others.

The Lost Sheep

—EVERYBODY OUGHT TO KNOW—

"Everybody ought to know who Jesus is."

from
MATTHEW 18:10-14;
LUKE 15:4-7

Jesus told His disciples a story. He wanted to teach them that God wants everyone to go to heaven. "If you had a hundred sheep and one was lost, what would you do? Wouldn't you leave the ninety-nine sheep in the meadow and look until you found the lost one? And when you found him, what would you do? Wouldn't you call your friends and say, 'Let's be happy, for I have found my lost sheep!' " Jesus said, "In the very same way, there is much happiness in heaven when one lost sinner comes to the Lord."

156

Lost people need to know about Jesus.

Jesus wants everyone to believe in Him.

I will tell people about Jesus.

The Prodigal Son

—I WILL SING OF THE MERCIES—

"I will sing of the mercies of the Lord forever."

from
LUKE 15:11-32

Jesus told this story: "A man had two sons. One day the younger son took his money and traveled to a far away land. There he wasted all his money. He took a job feeding pigs. At times, he was so hungry he even thought about eating some of the pig's food. Then he thought, "If I go home and say I'm sorry, maybe my father will let me work for food." He traveled back to his father's house. While the boy was still far from the house, his father saw him. He ran to meet him saying, "My son is home!" And he hugged and kissed his son. Jesus' story teaches us that God is our loving, forgiving Father.

God forgives us
when we ask Him.
The father forgave his son.

If I make bad choices, I will come back to my forgiving God.

Lazarus Lives

"I will, I will, I will heal My people."

from JOHN 11:1-44

A man named Lazarus was very sick. As he grew worse and worse, his family feared he might die. His sister Martha sent a message to Jesus. "Come quickly! Our brother, Lazarus, is very sick." But Jesus waited two days. When Jesus finally got there, Martha said, "Why didn't you come? Lazarus has died!" Jesus walked to the tomb where Lazarus lay. He shouted, "Lazarus, come out!" Suddenly Lazarus walked out of the tomb. God's timing was perfect. Lazarus was alive again!

God helps us at just the right time.
Lazarus lived again.

I will wait on Jesus. His timing is right for me.

Ten Sick Men

—COME BLESS THE LORD—

"Come bless the Lord, all ye servants of the Lord."

from
LUKE 17:11-19

As Jesus was traveling, he saw ten sick men who had a terrible disease called leprosy. The men called to Him, "Jesus, help us! Please make us well." What Jesus said next was very strange. He said, "Go and show yourselves to the priests." They were still sick, but because the ten men believed, they started walking toward the temple. As they went, the men began to feel better. With every step, they felt better and better. They were being healed. But only one man came back to thank Jesus. It is good to say thank you to Jesus!

It's good to give thanks to the Lord!

The healed man gave thanks to Jesus.

I will remember to say, "Thank You, Jesus."

Jesus Loves Children

—JESUS LOVES THE LITTLE CHILDREN—

"Jesus loves the little children, all the children of the world."

from
MATTHEW 19:13-14;
MARK 10:13-16;
LUKE 18:15-17

The boys and girls were so happy. They were going to meet Jesus! But when they came to the place where Jesus was teaching, His disciples stopped them. They said, "Jesus is an important man. He is too busy for children. Go away!" The children were sad. Then they heard Jesus say, "Let the children come to Me." He sat them on His lap and hugged them. Yes, Jesus loves the little children; He loves all the children of the world!

Jesus loves all children.
The children came to Jesus.

I will come to Jesus because He loves me.

Zacchaeus

—ZACCHAEUS—

"Zacchaeus was a wee little man, a wee little man was he."

from
LUKE 19:1-10

Jesus was coming to town. All the people wanted to see him. But Zacchaeus was not tall enough to see over the crowds. "How will I ever see Jesus?" he thought. "The crowds are tall and I'm so short!" Then Zacchaeus had an idea. "I'll climb a tall tree. Then I can see Jesus!" Sitting high on a branch, he could see Jesus walking down the road. As Jesus passed below, He stopped. Looking up into the tree He said, "Zacchaeus, come down. I will stay at your house today." That day, Jesus told Zacchaeus the Good News. And Zacchaeus gave his life to God.

Jesus wants us to know Him.

Zacchaeus wanted to know Jesus.

I won't let anything keep me from knowing Jesus.

Jesus, Our King

—SING HOSANNA—

"Sing hosanna to the King of kings!"

from
MATTHEW 21:1-9;
MARK 11:1-10;
LUKE 19:28-44

The people of Jerusalem were excited! Jesus was coming! They had heard His wonderful stories. They had seen His amazing miracles. As Jesus rode on a donkey into Jerusalem, a huge crowd stood along the road. They began to sing and shout. Many people spread their coats across the road before Him. Some waved palm branches as if to welcome a king! Together they shouted, "Hosanna to the King! Blessed is He who comes in the name of the Lord!" Yes, Jesus was coming. What a happy time it was!

It is good to praise Jesus.
All of Jerusalem praised Jesus.

I will sing and shout praises to Jesus, my King.

An Excellent Offering

—GIVE—

"Give and it will be given to you, my friend."

from
MARK 12:41-44;
LUKE 21:1-4

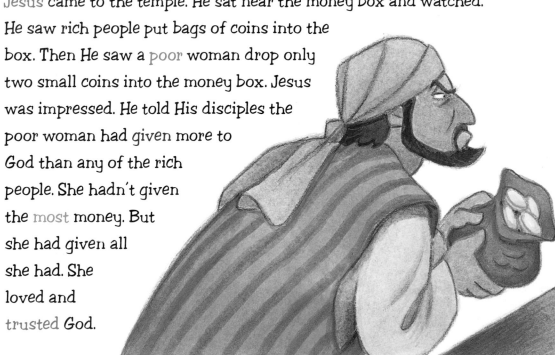

In Bible times, people went to the temple to worship God. Near the door was a money box where people put their offerings. One day, Jesus came to the temple. He sat near the money box and watched. He saw rich people put bags of coins into the box. Then He saw a poor woman drop only two small coins into the money box. Jesus was impressed. He told His disciples the poor woman had given more to God than any of the rich people. She hadn't given the most money. But she had given all she had. She loved and trusted God.

Our offering shows God we trust Him.

The woman gave an offering to God.

I will give to God.

Serving Others

"O how I love Jesus, because He first loved me."

from
JOHN 13:1-17

One evening Jesus and His disciples were eating dinner. It was a very happy time. He taught them many things about God. Then He stood up and wrapped a towel around His waist. He kneeled down and began washing their feet. He said that to be like Him we must help others. "This is what a good helper does," He said. "Do as I am doing. Serve others. You will be happy if you do."

To be like Jesus, we must help others.
Jesus served His disciples
by washing their feet.

I will help others to be like Jesus!

Last Supper

"I love Him better every D-A-Y. He is my Lord, the W-A-Y."

from
MATTHEW 26:17-28;
MARK 14:12-24;
LUKE 22:7-20; JOHN 13:1-34

Jesus ate a special supper with His disciples. He told them many things. Jesus took some bread and thanked God. Then He broke it and shared it with His disciples. Then He took a cup of wine and thanked God for it. He shared it too. He said, "Do this to remember Me." Then He gave them a new rule. He told them, "Love each other. That's how people will know you love Me."

We show Jesus we love Him by loving others.

Jesus taught His disciples to love others.

I will remember Jesus by loving others.

The Way to Heaven

—I AM THE WAY—

"I am the way, the truth, and the life.
No one comes to the Father except through Me."

from JOHN 14:1-7

Jesus told His disciples He would soon leave to go to heaven. He told them not to worry. He was going to get a heavenly place ready for them. Then He would return and take them to their new heavenly home. But Thomas said, "Lord, we don't know where You are going. How can we know the way?" Jesus answered, "I am the way." Believing in Jesus leads us to heaven!

Jesus is the way to heaven.

Thomas believed Jesus was the way to heaven.

I believe Jesus is the way to heaven.

Jesus Dies

—INTO MY HEART—

"Into my heart, into my heart, come into my heart, Lord Jesus."

from
MATTHEW 27:35-50;
MARK 15:21-37;
LUKE 23:33-49; JOHN 19:17-37

It was a very sad day. The disciples did not know what to do. Mary was crying. They kept thinking about Jesus. They remembered all the wonderful things He had said and done. But today their hearts hurt. Soldiers put Jesus on a cross. They didn't believe He was God's Son. On the cross Jesus said, "My God forgive them." Then He died. Yes, it was a very sad day. But God wasn't finished. It was all in His plan to save us. In three days everything would change. His friends would soon be happy.

Jesus died so we might live.
Jesus forgave all of our sins.

I am thankful Jesus died for me.

Surprise—Jesus Is Alive!

—JESUS LOVES EVEN ME—

"I am so glad that Jesus loves me, Jesus loves even me."

from
MATTHEW 28:1-8;
MARK 16:1-7;
LUKE 24:1-12; JOHN 20:1-18

After Jesus died His friends buried Him in a cave called a tomb. Then they put a big stone in front to close it. But Jesus had a surprise for His friends. When Mary went to the tomb where Jesus was buried, the stone had been rolled away. She saw two angels. They told her Jesus wasn't there. "He's alive!" they said. Mary was so happy! She ran back to tell the disciples what she had seen. Jesus didn't stay dead! She told them, "Jesus is alive!"

Jesus is alive!
The tomb was empty!

I am happy that Jesus lives!

A Big Catch

"Peter, James, and John in a sailboat.
They fished all night and caught no fishes."

from
JOHN 21:3-7

One day Peter, James, and John went fishing. They threw their nets into the water and waited. They fished all night but caught no fish. In the morning, a man called from the shore, "Did you catch any fish?" When they told him they had not, He told them to throw their net on the right side of the boat. So they did. Suddenly, their net was full of fish! Then Peter knew who the man on the shore was. "It's Jesus!" he said. Peter was so glad that he jumped into the water and swam to Jesus.

182

Jesus will help us in all we do.
He helped Peter, James, and John catch fish.

I know Jesus will help me too.

Jesus Goes to Heaven

—J·E·S·U·S—

"There is a name I love to sing."

from
MATTHEW 28:16-20;
MARK 16:15-20;
LUKE 24:45-51; ACTS 1:8-11

Jesus' work on earth was done. His followers had seen Him die on the cross and come alive again. Jesus told them they should go everywhere and tell people about Him. Then He said, "Now I am going to live with My Father." His followers watched as Jesus rose up in the air until He disappeared into the clouds. His friends looked up into the sky for a long time. Someday Jesus will come back the same way the disciples saw Him leave.

184

Jesus is in heaven,
but He is coming again.

I will watch for Jesus to return.

Tell the Good News

"Get on board little children, there's room for many a more."

from
MATTHEW
28:16-20

Heaven is a happy place. That's why Jesus said, "Go to all the world and tell everyone the good news!" We should tell people who speak English. Tell those who speak Spanish. Tell them in Russian and Chinese too. This is a great big world and there are lots of people. But everyone needs to know that God loves them. That's good news! People who love Jesus will get to go to heaven someday. So let's tell everyone!

All people need to know about Jesus.

Jesus said to go and tell others about Him.

I will go and tell others about Jesus.

Peter Heals the Beggar

—SILVER AND GOLD HAVE I NONE—

"Silver and gold have I none, but such as I have give I thee."

from
ACTS 3:1-11

Once a poor man sat by the temple gates. He couldn't walk, so there he sat, day after day, begging for money. One day, Peter and John went to the temple. As they passed, the beggar cried out to Peter and John for money. Peter said, "We don't have any money. But we will give you what we do have." Peter took the man's hand and the man stood, walked, and then jumped! His legs were well! Then Peter said, "It is Jesus' power that made you well." All the people who saw it praised Jesus!

It is good to share Jesus' love with others.

Peter and John shared God's love
with a man who couldn't walk.

I will share the love of Jesus.

Saul Sees the Light

—WALKING WITH JESUS—

"Walking with Jesus, walking every day, all along the way."

from
ACTS 9:1-18

Jesus is the Son of God. People who believe this are called Christians. Saul didn't believe that Jesus was the Son of God. He went from city to city putting Christians in prison. One day as he was traveling on the road to Damascus, a bright light shined down on him. It was so bright that it blinded him. Then Saul heard a voice from heaven saying, "Saul, why are you so unkind to Me?" Saul asked, "Who are you?" The voice answered, "I am Jesus." Saul's life was changed.

Jesus can change your life.

When Saul became a Christian, his name became Paul to show others how much he had changed.

I will obey Jesus. I will be a Christian!

Paul and Silas in Prison

—GOD WORKS FOR THE GOOD—

"And we know that in all things,
God works for the good of those who love Him."

from
ACTS 16:19-24;
ROMANS 8:28

Have you ever received a letter from someone? Letters can bring good news. Paul wrote letters to Christians, and they were full of good news. Paul wrote that no matter what bad things happen to Jesus' followers, God is working for their good. Paul was once put in prison for doing good things. But even when he was locked in chains, Paul was happy. He knew that God was working for his good. We know that God is always helping people who love Him. That's very good!

In all that happens, God is working for our good.

Even when Paul was in prison, God
was working for his good.

I believe that God is working to help me.

God's Grace

—AMAZING GRACE—

"Amazing grace, how sweet the sound that saved a wretch like me."

from
ROMANS 10:9, 13;
EPHESIANS 2:8

The sound of a siren is a scary sound. It means danger. But the sound of a bird singing is sweet to our ears. The sound of popcorn popping is sweet to our mouth. But to our hearts, there's nothing sweeter than the sound of the word "grace." Paul wrote about grace in the Bible. Grace has a very simple meaning: God forgives us no matter what we've said or done. All we have to do is ask Him! God offers grace to everyone. He has grace for you and grace for me. God's grace is truly amazing!

God's grace is amazing!
He will forgive us for the bad things we do.

Thank you, God, for Your grace to me!

God's Great Big Love!

—DEEP AND WIDE—

"Deep and wide, deep and wide, there's a fountain flowing deep and wide."

from EPHESIANS 3:18-19

It's easy to measure the size of this book. All you need is a ruler. It's easy to measure the length of a long train. We can even measure the tallest building and the widest ocean. But who can measure how big God's love is? It's higher than the highest star and wider than east is from west. It fills the heavens from end to end. We can't measure it, but we can treasure it!

God's love is big!

God's love fills the heavens and the earth.

I am thankful for God's love.

Working for Jesus

"Whatever, whatever you do, work at it with all your heart."

from COLOSSIANS 3:23

Some jobs can be lots of fun. Helping Dad wash the car is fun. Helping Mom bake a cake is fun too. But some jobs are not much fun. Cleaning your room can be boring. Picking up dirty socks can be awful. But Paul wrote in the Bible that whether a job is fun or not, we should do our very best. We should work as if we were washing God's car or baking God a cake or even picking up God's socks. Do your best, always!

God wants us to do our best.
Jesus always did His best.

I will always do my best!

The Bible Is True

—THE B·I·B·L·E—

"The B·I·B·L·E, yes that's the book for me!"

from
2 TIMOTHY 3:14-16

Paul wrote a letter to his friend Timothy. In it he said that all the verses in the Bible are true. God gives us the Bible to teach us how to live good lives. It tells us that Jesus is God's Son. It teaches us how to treat other people. It shows us the way to heaven. Yes, the Bible is a very special book. It is God's Word!

The Bible is a special book from God.
God's Word is true.

I will read my Bible and know it is true.

Jesus Is Knocking

—BEHOLD, BEHOLD—

"Behold, behold, I stand at the door and knock, knock, knock."

from
REVELATION 3:20

Knock, knock, knock! Have you ever heard that sound? Sure you have! It's the sound of someone knocking on a door. When you hear that sound, you go to the door to see who is knocking. Jesus once said that your heart is like a door. He stands at the door of your heart and knocks. He wants you to invite Him into your heart. If you feel Jesus knocking, let Him in!

Jesus wants you to invite Him in.

Jesus knocks on the door of your heart.

I will invite Jesus to come into my heart.

Heaven

"Oh, you can't get to heaven on roller skates."

from
REVELATION 21-22

The Bible says that heaven is a very special place. It's special because it is God's home! All of the angels live there too. The streets there are made of gold and shine like glass. A heavenly river is there with water as clear as crystal. The gates of heaven are made of beautiful pearls. The walls shine with jewels. But most importantly, Jesus is there! People who love and trust in Jesus will meet Him there. We will walk and talk with Him. We will share His love and joy forever in heaven. Heaven is a wonderful place!

God made heaven for those He loved.
Jesus lives in heaven.

I love Jesus so I will live forever with Him.

what he called the Third Section.

"That reincarnation of the Oprichnina lasted until 1917, when the Bolsheviks renamed it the All-Russian Extraordinary Commission for the Suppression of Counterrevolution and Sabotage — acronym Cheka."

"That sounds as if you're saying that the Czar's secret police just changed sides, became Communists," D'Alessandro said.

It was his first comment during the long history lesson.

"My son, you're saying two things, you realize," the archbishop said. "That the Oprichnina changed sides is one. That the Oprichnina became Communist is another. They never change sides. They may have worked for different masters, but they never become anything other than what they were, members of the Oprichnina."

"Excuse me, Your Eminence," D'Alessandro said, "but I've always been taught that the Russian secret police, by whatever name, were always Communist. Wasn't the first head of the Cheka — Dzerzhinsky — a lifelong Communist? I've always heard he spent most of his life in one Czarist jail or another before the Communist revolution. That's not so?"

"The Dziarzhynava family was of the

122

Second. The Czar said he was going to abdicate and, to that end, had already moved out of Moscow. He posted copies of the letter on walls and, importantly, in every church.

"The people, the letter said, could now run Russia to suit themselves, starting by picking a new Czar, to whom they could look for protection. This upset everybody. The people didn't want a new Czar who was not chosen by God. The boyars knew that picking one of their own to be the new Czar was going to result in a bloodbath. The officer corps knew that the privileges they had been granted were almost certainly not to be continued under a new Czar, and that the boyars would want their serfs back.

"The Czar was begged not to abdicate, to come home to Moscow. After letting them worry for a while, during which time they had a preview of what life without Czar Ivan would be like, he announced his terms for not abdicating.

"There would be something new in Russian, the Oprichnina — 'Separate Estate' — which would consist of one thousand households, some of the highest nobility of the boyars, some of lower-ranking boyars, some of senior military officers, a few of members of the merchant class, and even a few

119

families of extraordinarily successful peasants.

"They all had demonstrated a commendable degree of loyalty to the Czar. The Oprichnina would physically include certain districts of Russia and certain cities, and the revenue from these places would be used to support the Oprichnina and of course the Czar, who would live among them.

"The old establishment would remain in place. The boyars not included in the Oprichnina would retain their titles and privileges; the council — the *Duma* — would continue to operate, its decisions subject of course to the Czar's approval. But the communication would be one way. Except in extraordinary circumstances, no one not an Oprichniki would be permitted to communicate with the Oprichnina.

"The Czar's offer was accepted. God's man was back in charge. The boyars had their titles. The church was now supported by the state, so most of the priests and bishops were happy. Just about everybody was happy but Philip the Second, Metropolitan of Moscow, who let it be known that he thought the idea of the Oprichnina was un-Christian.

"The Czar understood that he could not tolerate doubt or criticism. And so Ivan set out for Tver, where the Metropolitan lived. On the way, he heard a rumor that the people and the administration in Russia's second-largest city, Great Novgorod, were unhappy with having to support Oprichnina.

"Just as soon as he had watched Metropolitan Philip being choked to death in Tver, the Czar went to Great Novgorod, where, over the course of five weeks, the army of the Oprichnina, often helped personally by Ivan himself, raped every female they could find, massacred every man they could find, and destroyed every farmhouse, warehouse, barn, monastery, church, every crop in the fields, every horse, cow, and chicken."

He paused, then said, "And so was born what we now call the SVR."

"Excuse me?" Jake Torine asked. "I got lost just now."

"Over the years, it has been known by different names, of course," the archimandrite explained. "It actually didn't have a name of its own, other than the Oprichnina, a state within a state, until Czar Nicholas the First. After Nicholas put down the Decembrist Revolution in 1825, he reorganized the trusted elements of the Oprichnina into original one thousand families in Ivan's Oprichnina," the archbishop said. "Felix Edmundovich Dzerzhinsky, the first head of the Cheka, was born on the family's estate in western Belarus. The estate was never confiscated by the Bolsheviks or the Mensheviks or the Communists after they took power. The family owns it to this day."

The archimandrite picked the narrative up.

"The Czar's Imperial Prisons were controlled by the Third Section. How well one fared in them — or whether one was actually in a prison, or was just on the roster — depended on how well one was regarded by the Oprichnina. The fact that the history books paint the tale of this heroic revolutionary languishing, starved and beaten, for years in a Czarist prison cell doesn't make it true."

The archbishop took his turn by asking, "And didn't you think it was a little odd that Lenin appointed Dzerzhinsky to head the Cheka and kept him there when there were so many deserving and reasonably talented Communists close to him?"

D'Alessandro put up both hands in an admission of confusion.

"The Cheka," the archimandrite went on, "was reorganized after the counterrevolution of 1922 as the GPU, later the OGPU. A man named Yaakov Peters was named to head it. By Felix Edmundovich Dzerzhinsky, who was minister of the interior, which controlled the OGPU.

"Dzerzhinsky died of a heart attack in 1926. After that there were constant reorganizations and renaming. In 1934, the OGPU became the NKVD — People's Commissariat for State Security. In 1943, the NKGB was split off from the NKVD. And in 1946, after the Great War, it became the MGB, Ministry of State Security."

"What you're saying, Your Grace," D'Alessandro said, "is that this state within a state . . ."

"The Oprichnina," the archimandrite furnished.

". . . the *Oprichnina* was in charge of everything? Only the names changed and the Oprichnina walked through the raindrops of the purges they had over there at least once a year?"

"My son," the archbishop said, "you're again putting together things that don't belong together. Yes, the Oprichnina remained — *remains* — in charge. No, not all the Oprichniki managed to live through all the purges. Enough did, of course, in order to maintain the Oprichnina and learn from the mistakes made."

"Excuse me, Your Eminence," Torine asked. "Are you saying the Oprichnina exists today?"

"Of course it does. Russia is under an Oprichnik."

"Putin?" D'Alessandro blurted.

"Who else," the archbishop replied, "but Vladimir Vladimirovich Putin?"

"And that Mr. Pevsner, Swe . . . Svetlana, and Colonel Berezovsky were — are — Oprichniki?"

Nicolai Tarasov raised his pudgy hand above his bald head.

When Torine looked at him, Tarasov said, smiling, "Yes, me, too. I confess. If there were membership cards, I would be a card-carrying Oprichnik."

"How do you get to be an Oprichnik?" D'Alessandro asked. "Like the Mafia makes 'made men'? First you whack somebody, then there's a ceremony where you cut your fingers to mingle blood, and then take an oath of silence?"

"One is born into the Oprichnik," the archbishop said. "Or, in the case of women, marries into it. Only very rarely can a man become an Oprichnik by marrying into it. There is no oath of silence, such as the Mafia oath of Omertà, because one is not

125

necessary. It is in the interest of every Oprichnik to keep what he or she knows about the state within the state from becoming public knowledge."

"May I have your permission, Your Eminence, to make a comment?" Aleksandr Pevsner asked. It was the first time he'd said anything.

The archbishop nodded.

"But please, my son, try to not get far off the subject," he said.

"The Oprichnina has not endured for more than four hundred years without difficulty," Pevsner said. "From time to time, it has been necessary to purify its membership —"

"Purify it? How was that done, Mr. Pevsner?" Jake Torine asked.

"I recently found it necessary to purify my personal staff of a man — an American — who betrayed the trust I placed in him."

"Howard Kennedy?" Torine asked.

Pevsner did not respond directly, but instead said, "As I was saying, we have found it necessary to purify our ranks from time to time and also to place under our protection certain individuals who have rendered one or more of us — and thus the Oprichnina — a great service.

"This was the case with our Charley.

Before he met Svetlana and Dmitri, I very seriously considered eliminating him as a threat. God in His never-failing wisdom stayed my hand, and Charley lived to save my life at the risk of his own. Knowing that others, in particular Vladimir Vladimirovich, still wanted our Charley out of the way, I sent word to Vladimir Vladimirovich that I considered our Charley my brother.

"Ordinarily, that would have been enough to protect our Charley, as a friend of the Oprichnina, but Vladimir Vladimirovich apparently decided that our Charley posed a threat he could not countenance and/or that I no longer had the authority to categorize Charley as a protected friend of the Oprichnina.

"He sent Dmitri and Svetlana to eliminate our Charley in Marburg, Germany. That operation turned out disastrously for Vladimir Vladimirovich, as you all know. Not only did Dmitri and Svetlana decide not to eliminate our Charley, but enlisted his aid in helping them to defect.

"Vladimir Vladimirovich had SVR agents waiting in Vienna to arrest Dmitri and Svetlana. Instead, our Charley flew them to Argentina and ultimately brought them here."

"Can I jump in here, Your Eminence?" Vic

D'Alessandro asked.

"I was afraid this would happen," the archbishop asked. "But yes, my son, you may. Try to be brief."

"Thank you," D'Alessandro said.

"Dmitri —"

"Please call me Tom, Vic."

"Okay. *Tom,* why did you defect? From all I've ever heard, all the intelligence services in Russia live very well, and I'm guessing that you Oprichniks lived pretty high on the hog. So why did you defect?"

"Because we came to the conclusion that sooner or later, Mr. Putin was going to get around to purifying us. We knew too much. We had family members — Aleksandr and Nicolai — who had, Vladimir Vladimirovich could reasonably argue, already defected."

"I don't think Vladimir Vladimirovich, if he could get his hands on us, would have actually fed us to starving dogs or thrown us off the Kremlin wall," Aleksandr Pevsner said, "but keeping us on drugs in a mental hospital for the rest of our lives seemed a distinct possibility."

"What did he have . . . does he have . . . against you?"

"You didn't tell them, Charley?" Pevsner asked.

Castillo shook his head.

"Would you have told them if they asked?" Pevsner asked.

"If they had a good reason for wanting to know, I would have."

"You really have the makings of a good Oprichnik," Pevsner said. "Well, now there is that reason, so I will tell them.

"In the former Union of Soviet Socialist Republics, I was a *polkovnik* — colonel — in both the Soviet Air Force and the SVR. I was in charge of Aeroflot operations world-wide, both in a business sense and in the security aspect. These duties required me to travel all over the world, and to make the appropriate contacts. My cousin Nicolai was my deputy in both roles.

"When the USSR collapsed, the SVR — which is to say Vladimir Vladimirovich — learned the new government had the odd notion that the assets of the SVR should be turned over to the new democratic government."

"What assets?" Torine asked.

"Would you believe tons of gold, Jake?" Castillo asked.

"Jesus Christ!" Torine said.

"Now *that* was blasphemous," the archbishop said.

"I'm sorry, Your Eminence," Torine said.

"You need Our Savior's forgiveness, not mine."

"Plus some tons of platinum," Castillo said, chuckling. "Not to mention a lot of cash."

Pevsner, his tone making it clear that he didn't appreciate contributions from others while he was explaining things, then went on:

"As I was saying. When Vladimir Vladimirovich was faced with the problem of not wanting to turn over the SVR's assets to the new democratic government, he turned to me. Nicolai and me. He correctly suspected that we would know how to get these assets out of Russia to places where they would be safe from the clutching hands of the new government.

"At about this time, Nicolai and I realized there were some aspects of capitalism we had not previously understood. As Ayn Rand so wisely put it — she was Russian, I presume you know — 'No man is entitled to the fruits of another man's labor.'

"So Nicolai and I told Vladimir Vladimirovich we would be happy to accommodate him for a small fee. Five percent of the value of what we placed safely outside the former Soviet Union."

"Jake," Castillo said, "you've always been

good at doing math in your head. Try this: In 1991, when the USSR collapsed, gold was about $375 an ounce. How much is five percent of two thousand pounds of gold, there being sixteen ounces of gold in each pound?"

"My Go— goodness," Torine said.

" 'Goodness' being a euphemism for God," the archbishop said, "there are those, myself included, who consider the phrase blasphemous."

"Again, I'm sorry, Your Eminence," Torine said, then looked at Castillo. "And you said 'tons of gold'? Plural?"

"So now you know," Castillo said, "where ol' Aleksandr got the money to buy Karin Hall, and all those cruise ships, and the Grand Cozumel Beach and Golf Resort, et cetera, et cetera."

"We started out with a couple of old transports from surplus Air Force stock," Pevsner said. "We flew surplus Soviet arms out of Russia, and luxury goods — Mercedes-Benz automobiles, Louis Vuitton luggage, that sort of thing — in.

"Mingled with the arms on the flights out of Moscow were fifty-five-gallon barrels of fuel. You would be surprised how much gold one can get into a fifty-five-gallon drum. That, unfortunately, is how I earned the reputation of being an arms dealer; but regretfully that was necessary as a cover. No one was going to believe I prospered so quickly providing antique samovars and Black Sea caviar to the world market.

"But turning to Vladimir Vladimirovich, who is really the subject of this meeting . . ."

"I'm so glad you remembered, my son," the archbishop said.

"As long as I have known Vladimir Vladimirovich, which has been for all of our lives, I always suspected — probably because of his father; the apple never falls far from the tree — that he was more of a Communist than a Christian, which means that he was far more interested in lining his pockets than promoting the general welfare of the Oprichnina."

"That characterization, I would suggest," the archbishop said, "qualifies as a rare exception to the scriptural admonition to 'judge not,' et cetera."

"I gather you are a Christian, Mr. Pevsner?" Naylor asked.

"Of course I'm a Christian," Pevsner said indignantly. "I'm surprised our Charley didn't make that quite clear to you."

"It must have slipped his mind," Naylor said.

"Where was I?" Pevsner asked.